Going Places

—

Elaine Fowler Palencia

FUTURECYCLE PRESS

www.futurecycle.org

Published by FutureCycle Press
Lexington, Kentucky, USA

ISBN 978-1-942371-09-0

For Michael, Jack, and Charlie Harper

Contents

The Big Woods

A flea market stands
along the old road
edging the woods
you played in as a child.
You don't remember it being there
but then again you've been gone
longer than you ever meant to be.
Leaving the kids in the car
you rummage through
cracked dishes and clasp knives
Bic lighters and chainsaws
knit caps and plastic combs.
Amid old curtains, trowels
back copies of *Bass Fishing*
cookie tins, nuts, bolts
spanners, clocks, and screws
you find a single glass slipper
a small, red cape
a spinning wheel
with a bloody spindle
things you remember owning
when you were young
and when you ask
the old couple at the cashbox
where they get their goods
they point to a gap
among the trees
where you glimpse
your children
following a trail
of breadcrumbs
into darkness
eating as they go.

First Memory, At Two Years

Grass smells my toes.
Shade cools me.
Sky is, and time.
Clouds shift.
Sun blares.
Cries, like a flock of birds wheeling
and I am scooped up by white arms.
The sun has lit my pinafore
spotted me under the spirea.
Lost, then found.
Scolded, then forgiven.
The pattern set for life.

Home for the Night

That childhood afternoon
I ran homewards through
late slanting light
sounds of sandlot ball
friendly supper smells.

Across backyards
my sturdy pony body pounded
ready to be brushed, fed
stabled for sleep.

Behind the house
across the street from ours
I looked up and saw
the tall back of the neighbors' house
blazing white gold.

Ahead, on our street
night had fallen.
Caught in the radiant present
my back warm with last light
I saw before me
deep in shadow, my home
already cloaked in the past

and understood for the first time:

I and
everyone I love
will die.
There is no escape
and nothing to do
but keep running towards the dark.

An August Day in Southern Ohio, 1851

A woman sits in a straight chair
on the porch of a clapboard farmhouse
snapping an apronful of pole beans
into a tin wash pan
and looking out on fields where distantly
under the brass clock of the sun
her husband is plowing with the mule.
In a cradle at her feet the baby sleeps
a dark curl sweated to his forehead.
She thinks of that November day last year
when her name was lifted into history
by a census taker recording for the first time
the names of the women and children
along with Head of Household.
Her age, too, was marked down, eighteen
and the place she was born
as if she mattered.
What a wonder, she thinks
that the government cares who I am!
People I will never see!

Just then
though the light does not change
she feels a shadow pass between her and the sun
as if a great bird is flying overhead, wings spread
and a chill rushes through her hair
as if a breeze is caught in it.
Now she recalls stories
the old residenters tell of the Shawnee
and how in those days, when you got the feeling
someone was watching
you paid attention to it.

She picks up the baby and the pan of beans
goes inside and shuts the door.

I sit back from my computer
pausing in my genealogical search
to touch her name on the screen.
She will have eleven more children.
Her husband will be shot in the face at Shiloh
and never be able to work the land again.
She will live to open the door
to four more census takers.
I rub my eyes and wait
for her to edge aside
a window curtain
and peep out.

An Only Child Tours the Library in Whitesburg, Kentucky

A visitor idly walking the shelves, tired
wondering who in town served the best coffee
I came upon volumes
of Kentucky birth statistics bound in black.

What a lark—look myself up, see if I existed.

Then I remembered another.
I'd never seen his name
never heard if he had one
had never seen a photo.
No one spoke of him
except once Mother said
"When your baby dies,
they move you out of the ward
put you in a room by yourself
don't want you upsetting the other new mothers."

I could stroll on
still keep forgetting him.

May 30, 1948, his birthday.

Named after our father.

His tiny hand waving at me through lines of print.

At a Coffee Shop in Berea, Kentucky,
Fall 2014

Coffee and croissants
beside a chilled window.
Outside, light snow.

Great-great-grandfather, today I awoke to your weather
and remembered how

you, a peaceable man summoned
                                to war
straggled past Berea
                    with the 52nd Georgia

(minus the captured
and the dead)

    this same month in 1862
                                in falling snow
                                        under the rod of Bragg

withdrawing from the failed
                        invasion of Kentucky.

You marched in thin clothes and broken shoes

    without water

    the parched corn running out

the cross of Vicksburg waiting beyond the unimaginable horizon.

Vera's House

Late morning sun stripes the beach
of spotless beige wall-to-wall.
Through an open window the Tennessee breeze
brings a dusty sugar smell of cut grass
stirring the satin-striped drapes.
In the nandinas a yellow warbler trills.
Vera lays a manicured hand on my shoulder
asks me to play the sparkling spinet
and I do, my own adolescent arrangement
of "Smoke Gets in Your Eyes"
as the two women, my mother
and the surviving sister of the man
she should have married, sit beaming
on the chintz sofa. Afterward Vera serves
coffee and Mexican wedding cookies
using her mother's blue-sprigged china.
At the door she hugs my mother and says
"Call me again if you're ever in town.
I'd like for you to meet my husband.
Oh, it's so good to see you
after all these years. You were the one
the whole family wanted."
They're both gone now.
My mother can never say what went wrong
but I remember thinking, as we left Vera's house
that this was the real America
and we were only visitors
from the kingdom of my father.

Georgia on His Mind

He was better in arithmetic, she in spelling
when they were classmates
at the one-room school in Nine Mile Hollow.
Dead of TB at twenty-three
she was the love of his life.
When the mood was on him, he'd cry
and tell this to my mother
or me, his only daughter.

We could see why he loved Georgia.
She never disappointed as we did.
An elderly neighbor told Mother
the dying girl always asked a friend
to be present when my future father
visited her sickbed. She didn't know what
to say to him, she complained, wishing
he wouldn't come. She was too sick to see
how much he needed her death
to excuse everything that would ever go wrong.

Mother Says

In 1954, Bill Monroe and the Blue Grass Boys
pick and sing at the drive-in outside of town.
Mother says
no child of mine
will be seen with the kind of people
who sweat bacon grease
and listen to tacky fiddlers.
The Stinson children from across the fence
come back home
with sequins and spangled fringe
stitched all over their clothes by the band's
glorious precise bowing.
Their mother laughs and says well
we can't afford new clothes otherwise.
In 1956, Jerry Lee Lewis
sends great balls of fire
streaking to the rafters of the high school gym.
Mother says
you must stay home to practice that Mozart, is that his name
and how you will curtsey at the end of your recital
as if you are meeting the Queen.
The Stinson kids come home
loaded like ivory hunters
with piano keys Jerry Lee
ripped out and flung at the audience.
Their mother says
Lord what I wouldn't give for one of Carl Perkins'
blue suede shoes.
In 1980, the Stinson kids come back to the Stinson Reunion
with good jobs, degrees, houses from here to France.

Mother says
why can't you be like them?
Why do you sit all day
turning the knobs on the radio?
What is it you're listening for?

Bluegrass Band

Headlong from the git-go they smack down
sidemeat sizing in an iron skillet
blackberry canes riffling the wind
train whistle rifling grooves on a mountain
snowmelt sluicing over sassafras roots
(that old boy on the washboard bass
isn't he some tall drink of water).
Rain plinks on tar roofs, tin roofs
on smoke-smelling cabins cold as kraut.
Granny women fry up hominy and johnnycakes
tow-headed kids call sooey pig sooey
axe rings on oak, ash, hickory
(stubble-chinned, long-haired guitar player
moving easy as a bent-willow rocker).
Thick thumbs strum ironhead
muskies lurking in the tailwaters
fiddler wails out shaped note singing
on Sunday morning after Saturday night drinking
(Son, the way he fills those sprayed-on jeans).
Soon they settle into medieval sounds
scything, riving, hoeing, adzing
metal on wood
wood on stone
leather on skin
yee-ha!
Red-faced newborn preacher shouting
needles flashing in calico quilt tops
fingerwork soft as rabbits in springtime
sad as blueticks baying at the moon.
Big-bellied mandolin man is keening
like a circular saw chewing into buckshot
picking gently as a blindfolded jeweler.

Bow-legged banjoer grinning like a possum
pours new pennies down a tall metal silo.

"Listen here," says a big busty woman
to her gum-snapping friend—
"after the show
we need to get to *know*
these boys."

To the Deer Parked Outside Big Lots

Maybe you know
three-point buck
what item was so urgently needed
as to leave you sprawled
on your back, hanging
out of the trunk of a Chevy Lumina
while the driver shopped

and the males of the human herd
crowded round to gawk
and urge their children
to take photos on their phones

your back hoofs daintily aligned
and pointed to the left
your front legs wrapped across each other
as if against a chill
your noble tawny chest
swelled in the final dream
like the breasts of a murdered odalisque
glimpsed between bedroom curtains.

Lincoln in the Afterlife

More tired than ever he felt
as a young lawyer riding
a twelve-thousand-square-mile circuit
nowadays Lincoln nods off
in his chair after dinner
worn out by overseeing
enterprises bearing his name
cities, schools, parks
monuments, museums, motels.
On Saturdays
rather than argue politics
with Washington, Jefferson, Jackson
under a spreading oak he plays pinochle
with Chief Blackhawk.
The Chief has fewer concerns
a college in Wisconsin, a hockey team
a restaurant in Chicago
and shares with Lincoln
an affinity for sorrow.
He has time to talk
as long as Lincoln wants
of the prairie in flower
of the ring of an axe in winter woods
and of how the sunlight glinted
off the rivers of Illinois
when both were too small as yet
to be caught in Destiny's fine net.

Scandalous

Driving north on I-39 in Illinois
the way the land keeps flattening
the horizontal sucking the vertical into itself
opening to the sky like an empty woman
who dominates by wanting.

I'm not used to this abandon.
I'm from Kentucky where the hills
know how to keep their knees together.

Mile after mile the road ticks
into the heart of time—
that cosmic manifestation
often mistaken for deity.

Later the highway rises with the land
offering the traveler
to the blank blue
like a sacrifice.

I can see eternity from here.
It is empty.
I want to go home

but the ground drifts differently
and I am gathered
into the dovetailing
grain-filled breasts
of Wisconsin.

Illinois Skies

Coming from a tight valley
in Kentucky hills
I knew nothing of
big sky theater, of
how the sky becomes
a silver-scaled fish that takes
a whole day to pass overhead

vast workaday skies
covering America's breadbasket
like a napkin made
from a chambray work shirt

pufferbelly clouds
taller than skyscrapers
eternity visible

dawns wider than longing
orange sunsets lingering
like the last organ chord
of Armageddon.

Now I live where
storm weather
threatens from Missouri
a gray limestone shelf
rising into periwinkle afternoon
like an important idea everyone
has forgotten until now

that we are birds
swiftly passing
swiftly gone
without changing
the color of the sky.

A Woman's Place

Jesus-blazoned tour bus rolls
into McDonald's parking lot

emits a gaseous sigh
and a line of pilgrims walking two by two.

Inside, the women take their places
at the counter to order food

while their pale spouses
nest at the tables and wait

to be fed, their mouths
moving in faint vestigial memory

of the evolutionary stage
in which they sported feathers.

The Caryatids of Appalachia

Small-town, hill-farm
aunts and grandmothers
who spoke in fossils
and smiled out of faces
weathered like sandstone
the limestone drape of their dresses
stark against the trees.
They chiseled lives out of flint
and ground their bones for bread.
Now they are gone under granite.
Their carven names alone remain
and every name a poem:
Agnes Emeline, Sarah Caldonia
Lillie Fay, Rilma Glenith, Victoria Jane—
the list goes on of mountain women
who held up the sky.

Eastern Kentucky Road

Winding, twisting, black as a snake
between blue hills, a sliver of lake
dogwood, redbud, wild carrot and garlic
terrapin slow-coach bound for a frolic
Pentecostal church, tin-roofed shack
walnut, chinquapin, basswood, sumac
old barn, new barn, bridge over creek
sweet gum, broom sedge, laurel, beech
red clover, pine, bantams in a flock
fence of black locust
hickory, chickory, dock.

Along Route 23

When you venture toward home
the old ones will be waiting for you.
In the bathroom mirror
of a Huddle House in eastern Kentucky
my late grandmother has been biding her time
the gravity of decades lengthening
the lobes of her ears
flesh tightening over her high cheekbones.
When I look up from washing my hands
our eyes meet and I recognize
the gentle, bewildered smile
of an innocent nature
struggling day after day
against darkness.
That smile is mine now.
Neither of us can believe
what has become of me.

Confessing to James Still

Down from Dead Mare Branch
to flog your poems at a book fair
tired and inconvenienced
you sat in a corner
at the authors' reception
spitting fireballs.

"Know how all these people got here?
They wrote cookbooks!"

"The Agrarians?
The Agrarians did their farming on paper!"

Mr. Still, I need to tell you
I once ghostwrote a cookbook
gained five pounds testing the recipes
and thought I'd grown into a writer.

And worse:
I come from farmers who sold their farms.
My country aunt said Mother
never taught me to work hard
and she's right, if you mean hoeing corn.
I farm on paper, too
herding dictionary animals
chasing similes with a butterfly net
not knowing a Roma bean
from a Kentucky Wonder.

Nevertheless
a writer-farmer such as yourself
must know how hard it is
to find newground in writing

and how much sweat it takes
to plant a decent crop
and bring it to harvest.
As for the gone farms
I can always read about them
in the encyclopedia
under the heading *Eden.*

Little Brother

The balsam woolly adelgid
sap-sucking secreter
one thirty-secondth of an inch long
has never studied aesthetics
or political philosophy and so
knows nothing of the lovely view
or Locke's social contract.

As did we all
it started life elsewhere
and came to these shores
in search of more.
Enterprising, it dedicates itself
to culinary excellence
preferring slow food to fast
fresh to canned.

Wily hunter and gatherer
it kills what it eats.
It has made ghost forests
of the Fraser firs
turned parts of the Smokies
into a thicket of gray sticks.

Do not blame it
for assuming it owns the forest
for living as if the forest
exists to sustain it.
Little brother adelgid
though you walk the land
in boots of fire
still we are more deadly.
Watch us behead a mountain
to steal its coal.

Appalachian Out-Migration

You see them along the roads at night now
walking single file out of the graveyards
wraith-women carrying stillborn babies
war veterans wearing the medals
they were buried with
the usual motorcycle accidents
innocents done in by old age
crushed miners and coal truck road kill.

Once you remove the mountains
even the dead won't stay.
Soon the elk they've trucked in to distract us
from the desecration
can drink the polluted water in peace
and breed like cancer.

Going Places

The summer he turned eighteen, in 1903
Grandpa ventured north from Gallia County
to work on a farm outside Springfield, Ohio
a hundred and fifty miles from home.
He returned with money in his pockets
to marry and buy a back-break hill farm
across the river in West Virginia.
Talked about the trip for the rest of his life.
The big fields. The reapers. The combines.
The tedders for haying.
He came home confirmed in his belief
that hard work was the answer.
It had taken him places.
He was now a man who'd seen the world.
But if he really applied himself
to clearing the pastures, timbering
milking, haying, and raising corn
he would never have to leave home again.

Crossing Over

Mother and Daddy knew laundry
was the way out of the hills
so every Saturday night they boiled water
to fill the big galvanized tub in the kitchen
and scalded their hill speech, scrubbed out
the diphthongs, the barnyard similes
the Chaucerian echoes and localisms
and starched their talk stiff as a Methodist preacher's shirt.

But when they got into their nineties
the people hiding in their bones re-took their tongues.
"Come hyere, your dress is sigogglin'," Mother said.
Daddy said, "I'm of a mind to see the graves across the Ohio.
I'll git Sheephead Short t'overboat us, how's that grab ye?"

Sheephead had drowned in the thirties
but I believed Daddy, believed we'd get there.

Carrying the Farm

When he left the one-room school in the hollow
for high school in town
the farm insisted on going along.
It fit in his pocket
snug as a buckeye
ninety acres of West Virginia hillside
and a creek flaring with sunfish.

When he took the bus to college
returning each night to chores
and midnight homework
upstairs in the old log house
the farm had grown so big
he needed a rucksack to take it to class—
it insisted on going.

When he left home for further study
the farm took up the whole steamer trunk
his mother had brought to her marriage.
There was no room for the brother
drinking himself to death
the sister who had run away from home
the parents with eighth-grade schooling.

When he married an educated woman
although she came from country people
she made the farm stay outside the house.
It lurked around the japonica bushes, sulking
and flinging mud on the sidewalk.

When he became a college teacher
the farm settled on the roof
like a rock shelf.

At night it scattered his teaching notes
murmured to him of bad faith and abandonment.

When he and his city-loving sister
sold the farm it gnashed its rocks
and groaned deep in its ravines
welling to a great blue bruise over the neighborhood
its manure breath hot on the back of his neck.

When he retired from teaching
the farm required him to replace
his suit and tie with overalls
and expand his garden.
He had no time for anything
but planting and hoeing
and acquiring his father's rheumatism.

When he lay boneless
in the last nursing home, the farm
swaying lower and lower
over his bed, dirt sifting from
its underside, opened its gates
and beckoned him in.

Finding the Graves

Black iron eagles
guard the cemetery gates.
Rain approaches
over the Chilhowees.
The wind smells
of wood smoke.
We have driven hours
to find the ancestors
Mother and I.
Winter pneumonia
has made her anxious
for addresses of the dead.
From the car
she points me down rows
and I step lively, I tell you
among sunken, reaching mounds.
"Try there, or there," she gasps.
"When Mama died
I parked under a cedar
that shed on the car."
Down the necroavenues
I lope ahead of the rain
veering from cedar to cedar
scanning the stones
assuming my mother's mantle
of kin-keeper, grave-knower.
A rooster crows far off
maybe as distant
as Grandpa's barn
gone these thirty years.
"They were on a hill," she cries
as I trot between the raindrops.

"When I'm gone
no one will know
but you."
The rain is dragging
night over us
when I find them
ranged as in a church pew
Grandpa, Grandma, Aunt Louise
Uncle George, Aunt Dorothy, Cousin John
and down the slope
Uncle Claude, Aunt Jessie, Cousin William.
"Come and see," I call.
"Don't need to," she whispers.
Homeward bound on a winding road
caught in the storm's black fury
she wakes: "Anybody believes in heaven
is just crazy. We're animals. Die like them.
I'm not afraid."
Sleeps again, to wake laughing.
"There's a man sitting beside me."
"Where?"
"Here by the window."
"Who?"
"Don't know. Dark-haired.
A friendly presence."
Lightning splits the rain
into jagged silver
turns her into a white wraith.
There is no other car on the road
and the center line is gone.
We could die here, now.
I lean over the wheel
straining to tell
the side of a mountain
from a hole in the ground.

Home Visits

I'm there at all hours
more and more often
as I get older
unbeknownst
to the current owners
who have never heard of me.

I bathe in the claw-footed tub
they ripped out years ago
sprinkle brown sugar
on my oatmeal in the kitchen
lie in my long-gone childhood bed
on humid summer nights
watching fireflies flash in the garden.

At times the occupants
may feel a breeze
in the upstairs hall
see a shadow fall
across a sunlit floor
hear a creak on the basement stairs
wake from an uneasy dream
in which their furniture
is being repossessed.

Near the Kentucky-Virginia Border, Early Autumn

The past beats in me like a second heart.
The blacktop goes up and up the mountain.
Kudzu has smothered the road signs and a school bus.
It has choked the creek and is rappelling across the road
on an electrical wire.
In a hairpin bend nestles the Big Flea, selling
pigs, chickens, rabbits, iron skillets, funerary urns
funnel cakes, water-damaged paperbacks, cornmeal, guns.
I'm not from around here anymore.
The little white churches in the hollows cross their arms
and look ashamed of how small their cemeteries are.
Coal trucks roar around the turns like sharks charging a rowboat.
In a local museum there is a Civil War exhibit
soldiers' photographs discovered
in the dead letter office, never delivered.
Twice dead, then, those pale-eyed young men.
The road goes up and up the mountain.
Mist smokes in the ravines.
In another silent museum lie letters
found next to the bodies of trapped miners.
Remember I love you and don't worry. I just went to sleep.
Boys be good and whatever you do don't become miners.
Night falls like a forest keeling over in a straight-line wind.
The lights of the prison on top of the mountain
take out the stars.

Supper on the Patio

Marinated chicken sings on the grill.
Bumblebees fumble in the lavender.
Next door, the neighbors play
a breathy jazz flute CD
music to strangle doves by.

Across the golf course
at an umbrella table
an old man eats alone.
I saw him up close once.
He is our age, or younger.

We sit at our table
under a striped umbrella.
For nearly fifty years
this is where we've been headed.
We're here now.

I hand you sliced tomatoes
on a white plate.
A rising wind flutters the yawning daylilies.
Tall clouds build in the blue.
Later there will be rain.

—

Acknowledgments

Appalachian Heritage: "The Caryatids of Appalachia"

Appalachian Journal: "Little Brother," "Going Places," "Confessing
 to James Still," "Carrying the Farm"

Back Home in Kentucky: "Eastern Kentucky Road"

Big Muddy: "Illinois Skies"

Encore: NFSPS Prize Poems 2003: "Bluegrass Band"

Heartland Review: "Scandalous"

Kentucky Review: "An August Day in Southern Ohio, 1851,"
 "An Only Child Tours the Library in Whitesburg, Kentucky"

Nerve Cowboy: "A Woman's Place," "To the Deer Parked Outside Big Lots"

Now and Then: "Appalachian Out-Migration"

Pegasus: "Lincoln in the Afterlife"

Pine Mountain Sand & Gravel: "Home for the Night"

Spoon River Poetry Review: "The Big Woods," "Mother Says"

Still: "Near the Kentucky-Virginia Border, Early Autumn,"
 "Along Route 23," "At a Coffee Shop in Berea, Kentucky, Fall 2014,"
 "Home Visits"

Zone 3: "Finding the Graves"

Special thanks to readers Michael Palencia-Roth and John Palen, whose
suggestions improved this collection.

*Cover photo, "At rest," and author photo by Vanda Galen; background art,
John Tillbrook's photo of "The Mackerel Sky," an original oil painting by
Kenneth Denton; cover and interior book design by Diane Kistner; Chaparral
Pro text and titling*

About FutureCycle Press

FutureCycle Press is dedicated to publishing lasting English-language poetry books, chapbooks, and anthologies in both print-on-demand and Kindle ebook formats. Founded in 2007 by long-time independent editor/publishers and partners Diane Kistner and Robert S. King, the press incorporated as a nonprofit in 2012. A number of our editors are distinguished poets and writers in their own right, and we have been actively involved in the small press movement going back to the early seventies.

The FutureCycle Poetry Book Prize and honorarium is awarded annually for the best full-length volume of poetry we publish in a calendar year. Introduced in 2013, our Good Works projects are anthologies devoted to issues of universal significance, with all proceeds donated to a related worthy cause. Our Selected Poems series highlights contemporary poets with a substantial body of work to their credit; with this series we strive to resurrect work that has had limited distribution and is now out of print.

We are dedicated to giving all of the authors we publish the care their work deserves, making our catalog of titles the most diverse and distinguished it can be, and paying forward any earnings to fund more great books.

We've learned a few things about independent publishing over the years. We've also evolved a unique, resilient publishing model that allows us to focus mainly on vetting and preserving for posterity the most books of exceptional quality without becoming overwhelmed with bookkeeping and mailing, fundraising activities, or taxing editorial and production "bubbles." To find out more about what we are doing, come see us at www.futurecycle.org.

www.ingramcontent.com/pod-product-compliance
Lightning Source LLC
Chambersburg PA
CBHW070117070426
42448CB00040B/3113